EDITED BY HELEN EXLEY

The Be Series was conceived and inspired by Emma Ashby.

Published in 2019 by Helen Exley ® LONDON in Great Britain.

Background wash illustrations by Angela Kerr,
motif illustration by Juliette Clarke.
© Helen Exley Creative Ltd 2019.

All the words by Charlotte Gray, Odile Dormeuil and
Pamela Dugdale © Helen Exley Creative Ltd 2019.
Design, selection and arrangement © Helen Exley Creative Ltd 2019.

The moral right of the author has been asserted.

ISBN 978-1-78485-199-6

12 11 10 9 8 7 6 5 4 3 2 1

OTHER BOOKS IN THE SERIES

Be Happy!   Be Confident!   Be You!

Helen Exley ® LONDON,
16 Chalk Hill, Watford, Herts WD19 4BG, UK
www.helenexley.com

Be Brave!

Helen Exley

The fact that courage
is expected of you
in the face of the unbearable
gives you strength
for the rest of your life.

NELSON ROLIHLAHLA MANDELA
1918 – 2013

All through my life I have been tested.
My will has been tested,
my courage has been tested,
my strength has been tested.
Now my patience and endurance
are being tested...
I have learned to live my life
one step, one breath,
and one moment at a time,
but it was a long road.
I set out on a journey
of love, seeking truth, peace,
and understanding.
I am still learning.

MUHAMMAD ALI 1942 – 2016

It's okay
to be scared.
Being scared means
you're about to do
something really,
really brave.

AUTHOR UNKNOWN

To develop courage
you have to start developing
courage as you do
any other muscle.
You have to start with
small things and build it up.

MAYA ANGELOU 1928 – 2014

Go out on a limb.
That's where the fruit is!

JIMMY CARTER, B. 1924

For people sometimes believed
that it was safer to live with complaints,
was necessary to cooperate with grief,
was all right to become
an accomplice in self-ambush...
Take heart to flat out decide
to be well and stride into the future
sane and whole.

TONI CADE BAMBARA 1939 – 1995

Everything
you've ever
wanted
is on
the other side
of fear.

GEORGE ADDAIR

Live to the point

I have always grown from my problems
and challenges, from the things
that don't work out,
that's when I've really learned.

CAROL BURNETT, B. 1933

of tears. ALBERT CAMUS 1913 – 1960

Courage is the most important
of all virtues,
because without courage
we can't practice any other virtue
with consistency.

MAYA ANGELOU 1928 – 2014

There is a stubbornness about me
that never can bear to be frightened
at the will of others.
My courage always rises at every attempt
to intimidate me.

JANE AUSTEN 1775 – 1817

You need to have faith in yourself.
Be Brave and Take Risks.
You don't have to have it all figured out
to move forward.

ROY T. BENNETT

You can defeat fear
through humour,
through pain,
through honesty,
bravery,
intuition,
and through love
in the truest sense.

JOHN CASSAVETES 1929 – 1989

Opportunity does not knock,
it presents itself
when you beat down the door.

KYLE CHANDLER, B. 1965

To dare is

to live.

SUZANNE C. COLE

It takes courage to grow up
and become who you really are.

E. E. CUMMINGS 1894 – 1962

You need
to have
sufficient
courage
to make
mistakes.

PAULO COELHO, B. 1947

One ought never to turn one's back
on a threatened danger
and try to run away from it.
If you do that, you will double
the danger. But if you meet it promptly
and without flinching,
you will reduce the danger by half.

SIR WINSTON CHURCHILL 1874 – 1965

Courage is being
the only one who knows
how terrified you are.

TOM CLANCY 1947 – 2013

Ships in harbor
are safe,
but that's not
what ships
are built for.

JOHN SHEDD

It's only the fear that we can't do better
that anchors us to a painful place.
Fear is our only enemy, our chain to misery
and heartache. Fear keeps us focused
on what we don't want rather than on
what we must do...
Being fearful is like living in a prison
without locks. We can open the gates
and step into the light any time we choose.

SUSAN L. TAYLOR, B. 1946

It takes courage to love, but pain through love is the purifying fire which those who love generously know. We all know people who are so much afraid of pain that they shut themselves up like clams in a shell and, giving out nothing, receive nothing and therefore shrink until life is a mere living death.

ELEANOR ROOSEVELT 1884 – 1962

I am not a courageous person by nature.
I have simply discovered that, at certain key
moments in this life, you must find courage
in yourself, in order to move forward
and live. It is like a muscle and it must
be exercised, first a little, and then more
and more. All the really exciting things
possible during the course of a lifetime
require a little more courage than we
currently have. A deep breath and a leap.

JOHN PATRICK SHANLEY

Fight till the

People are made of flesh and blood
and a miracle fibre called courage.

MIGNON MCLAUGHLIN 1913 – 1983

If you hear the dogs, keep going.
If you see the torches in the woods, keep going.
If there's shouting after you, keep going.
Don't ever stop. Keep going.
If you want the taste of freedom, keep going.

HARRIET TUBMAN 1820 – 1913

last gasp.

WILLIAM SHAKESPEARE 1564 – 1616

N o need to be ashamed
that you're afraid.
Only the stupid claim to know no fear.
Fear is not your enemy but a
wise companion, warning you of danger.
Take the warning and prepare
yourself – work steadily and face
whatever comes with courage.

ODILE DORMEUIL

Courage is being scared to death but saddling up anyway.

JOHN WAYNE 1907 – 1979

My own particular bugbear is FEAR. I seem to have been born with this inordinate amount of fear and, in the past, my mind became a master at concocting the most hair-raising scenes from what amounts to a tiny amount of storyline... but how do I deal with the fear? By allowing it, having no resistance, saying "Look, you too are welcome."

When I do this, it comes in like a cat and lies gently at my feet – when I resist, I think, Oh no, here it comes, look out. It forms

like a tiger that wants to trap me,
play games with me and fully devour me.
So sometimes I choose to let it devour me
and it sometimes feels like a fire burning
up my body and then it goes. When we can
finally allow WHAT is here to be here –
know that those emotions will not destroy us –
that we don't need to define ourselves by them
– thinking, Oh, I shouldn't feel anger, sadness,
frustration, whatever it is, we can finally allow
ourselves to "be."

CARON KEATING 1962 – 2004

There is glory in

The world has no room for cowards. We must all be ready somehow to toil, to suffer, to die. And yours is not the less noble because no drum beats before you when you go out into your daily battlefields, and no crowds shout about your coming when you return from your daily victory or defeat.

ROBERT LOUIS STEVENSON 1850 – 1894

a great mistake.

NATHALIA CRANE 1913 – 1998

A tree grows stronger,
subjected to the seasons
– the shifts in weather
from violence to calm,
from bitter cold
to overwhelming heat.
Take all that comes –
and use it wisely.

CHARLOTTE GRAY

No matter what happens,
keep on beginning and failing.
Each time you fail,
start all over again,
and you will grow stronger
until you find that you
have accomplished a purpose –
not the one you began with,
perhaps, but one
you will be glad to remember.

ANNE SULLIVAN 1866 – 1936

A fledgling,
teetering on the edge
of flight,
must summon up
its courage and launch
into the air.

PAMELA DUGDALE

Owning our story can be hard but not nearly as difficult as spending our lives running from it. Embracing our vulnerabilities is risky but not nearly as dangerous as giving up on love and belonging and joy – the experiences that make us the most vulnerable. Only when we are brave enough to explore the darkness will we discover the infinite power of our light.

BRENE BROWN, B. 1965

To be a success, you need more than just a competitive edge. You need a hide like a rhino, the ability to operate way outside normal comfort zones, a willingness to reinvent the rules, and total, utter, complete self-belief – against all odds.
If you don't believe you can do it, why should anyone else?

LORD ALAN SUGAR, B. 1947

You will never
do anything in this world
without courage.
It is the greatest
quality of the mind
next to honour.

ARISTOTLE 384 B.C. – 322 B.C.

Don't quit.
Suffer now and live
the rest of your life
as a champion.

MUHAMMAD ALI 1942 – 2016

Beware;
for I am fearless,
and therefore
powerful.

MARY WOLLSTONECRAFT SHELLEY
1797 – 1851

Sometimes
even to live
is an act
of courage.

SENECA THE YOUNGER
4 B.C. – A.D. 65

Some people won't be happy
until they've pushed you
to the ground.
What you have to do
is have the courage to stand
your ground and not give them
the time of day.
Hold on to your power
and never give it away.

DONNA SCHOENROCK

Fortune favours

Always bear in mind that your own resolution to succeed is more important than any other one thing.

ABRAHAM LINCOLN 1809 – 1865

You have to stand
for what you believe in and sometimes
you have to stand alone.

QUEEN LATIFAH, B. 1970

the bold. LATIN PROVERB

Courage has nothing to do
with your determination.
It has to do with what you decide
in that moment when you are called upon.
No matter how small that moment,
or how personal, it is a moment
when your life takes a turn
and the lives of those around you
take a turn because of you.

RITA DOVE

What matters
is not the size
of the dog
in the fight,
but the size
of the fight
in the dog.

DWIGHT D. EISENHOWER 1890 – 1969

If you play it safe in life you've decided that you don't want to grow any more.

SHIRLEY HUFSTEDLER 1925 – 2016

It is courage,
courage,
courage,
that raises
the blood of life
to crimson
splendour.

HORACE 65 B.C. – 8 B.C.

He who loses wealth
loses much;
but he who lose their courage
loses all.

MIGUEL DE CERVANTES 1547 – 1616

Courage is what it takes
to stand up and speak;
courage is also
what it takes to sit down
and listen.

Never give up,
because you never know
what the tide will bring
in the next day.

TOM HANKS, B.1956

What would you do if you weren't afraid?

SPENCER JOHNSON

Everyone including you
suffers when you refuse to be all
and do all you can.

FELA DUROTOYE, B. 1971

Courage and perseverance have a magical talisman, before which difficulties disappear, and obstacles vanish into air.

JOHN QUINCY ADAMS 1767 – 1848

Courage is about learning how
to function despite the fear;
to put aside your instincts to run
or give in completely to the anger
born from fear.
Courage is about using your brain
and your heart when every cell
of your body is screaming at you
to fight or flee – and then following
through on what you believe
is the right thing to do.

JIM BUTCHER

When a great adventure is offered, you don't refuse it.

First female to fly solo across the Atlantic Ocean.
AMELIA EARHART 1898 – 1937

Above all,
be the heroine
of your life,
not the victim.

NORA EPHRON, B. 1941

Courage is resistance
to fear, mastery of fear –
not absence of fear.

MARK TWAIN 1835 – 1910

Have enough
courage
to trust love
one more time
and always
one more time.

MAYA ANGELOU 1928 – 2014

Don't Make Assumptions.
Find the courage to ask questions and
to express what you really want.
Communicate with others as clearly
as you can to avoid misunderstandings,
sadness and drama.
With just this one agreement,
you can completely transform
your life.

DON MIGUEL RUIZ, B. 1952

Step into the unknown – live in it –
and be prepared to hang out there.
We cannot know what's in store for us,
and by hanging on to what's familiar we block
the new. Until hanging on by our fingertips
to the old life, fed up with prising off
our fingertips one by one, it simply kicks us
into the abyss. As we fall screaming,
it prepares a feather mattress for us.
Stunned, we wonder why we didn't dive off
to begin with. Live life.
There's no waiting game.
What is it you want to create right now?
How do you want to be?
Do it now.

CARON KEATING 1962 – 2004

Life only demands
from you
the strength
you possess.

DAG HAMMARSKJÖLD 1905 – 1961

I wanted you to see what real courage is,
instead of getting the idea that courage
is a man with a gun in his hand.
It's when you know you're licked
before you begin but you begin anyway
and you see it through no matter what.

HARPER LEE 1926 – 2016

Have the courage to say no.
Have the courage to face the truth.
Do the right thing because it is right.
These are the magic keys
to living your life with integrity.

W. CLEMENT STONE 1902 – 2002

I wanted a perfect ending.
Now I've learned, the hard way,
that some poems don't rhyme,
and some stories don't have
a clear beginning, middle, and end.
Life is about not knowing,
having to change, taking the moment
and making the best of it,
without knowing
what's going to happen next.

GILDA RADNER 1946 – 1989

Do one thing
every day
that scares you.

MARY SCHMICH

The person who
is not courageous enough
to take risks
will accomplish
nothing in life.

MUHAMMAD ALI 1942 – 2016

Do the hardest thing
on earth for you.
Act for yourself.

KATHERINE MANSFIELD 1888 – 1923

Bravery
is not
a quality
of the body;
it is of
the soul.

MAHATMA GANDHI 1869 — 1948

Some walks
you have to take alone.

SUZANNE COLLINS

The best way out is

Some people believe holding on
and hanging in there are signs
of great strength. However,
there are times when it takes much more
strength to know when to let go
and then do it.

ANN LANDERS 1918 – 2002

always through.

ROBERT FROST 1874 – 1963

A lot of people
are afraid to say
what they want.
That's why they don't get
what they want.

MADONNA, B. 1958

Courage is looking fear right
in the eye and saying,
"Get the hell out of my way,
I've got awesome things to do."

AUTHOR UNKNOWN

The successful know
that the road to success
is always under construction;
they understand
the roughness of it
and never expect it
to be smooth.

HERBERT O. NOBLEMAN

Failure isn't an option.
I've erased the word "fear" from
my vocabulary, and I think when you
erase fear, you can't fail.

ALICIA KEYS, B.1981

Life shrinks or expands i

proportion to one's courage.

ANAÏS NIN 1903 – 1977

Expose yourself to your deepest fear;
after that the fear of freedom shrinks
and vanishes. You are free.

JIM MORRISON

Only
in the
darkness
can you
see
the stars.

MARTIN LUTHER KING JR. 1929 – 1968

When you get into
a tight place and everything
goes against you,
till it seems as though
you could not hang on
a minute longer,
never give up then,
for that is just the place
and time
that the tide will turn.

HARRIET BEECHER STOWE 1811 – 1896

We believe in
ordinary acts of bravery,
in the courage
that drives one person
to stand up for another.

VERONICA ROTH, B. 1988

And only weaklings...
who lack courage...
when the whole world says
they're wrong, ever lose.

ZELDA FITZGERALD 1900 – 1948

Fear is not your enemy.
It is a compass pointing you
to the areas where
you need to grow.

STEVE PAVLINA

Our greatest
glory
is not in
never falling,
but in rising
every time
we fall.

CONFUCIUS 551 B.C. – 479 B.C.

It isn't for the moment
you are struck
that you need courage,
but for the long
uphill climb back
to sanity and faith
and security.

ANNE MORROW LINDBERGH
1906 – 2001

The most courageous act is still to think for yourself. Aloud.

COCO CHANEL 1883 – 1971

Perhaps all the dragons in our lives
are princesses who are only
waiting to see us act,
just once, with beauty and courage.

RAINER MARIA RILKE 1875 – 1926

No matter how bad
things got,
my mother made it clear
that we were not defined
by our financial situation.
We were defined
by our ability to overcome it.

ANNA PEREZ

Creativity requires
the courage to let go
of certainties.

ERICH FROMM 1900 – 1980

March on, and fear not the thorns,
or the sharp stones on life's path.

KAHLIL GIBRAN 1883 – 1931

Fly free. Fly high and far.
Your wings are strong.
There will be times
when much will be
asked of you.
I wish you the courage
and endurance
and the wisdom you need.

PAMELA DUGDALE

Physical bravery
is an animal instinct;
moral bravery
is much higher
and truer courage.

WENDELL PHILLIPS

It is not the critic who counts...
The credit belongs to the one who is actually
in the arena; whose face is marred by dust
and sweat and blood; who strives valiantly;
who errs and comes short again and again;
because there is not effort without error and
shortcoming; but who does actually strive
to do the deeds; who knows the great
enthusiasms, the great devotions; who spends
themself in a worthy cause; who, at the best,
knows in the end the triumph of high
achievement, and who, at the worst, if failure
comes, at least fails while daring greatly,
so that their place shall never be with those
cold and timid souls who know neither
victory nor defeat.

THEODORE ROOSEVELT 1858 – 1919

When I'm old and dying,
I plan to look back on my life
and say "Wow,
that was an adventure"
not "Wow, I sure felt safe."

TOM PRESTON-WERNER, B. 1979

Only one feat
is possible –
not to have to run away.

DAG HAMMARSKJÖLD 1905 – 1961

There's something
so vibrant and gutsy
about courage;
just do it.

ANITA RODDICK 1942 – 2007

Don't run away
when you are faced
with trouble.
Face it.
Deal with it.
Or you'll be running
all your life
in the wrong direction.

ODILE DORMEUIL

To believe yourself brave
is to be brave;
it is the one only
essential thing.

MARK TWAIN 1835 – 1910

In battle it is the cowards
who run the most risk;
bravery is a rampart of defence.

SALLUST

For what it's worth; it's never too late or, in my case, too early to be whoever you want to be. There's no time limit, stop whenever you want. You can change or stay the same, there are no rules to this thing. We can make the best or the worst of it. I hope you make the best of it. And I hope you see things that startle you. I hope you feel things you never felt before. I hope you meet people with a different point of view. I hope you live a life you're proud of. If you find that you're not, I hope you have the courage to start all over again.

ERIC ROTH

Courage
is rightly esteemed
the first of human
qualities...
because it is
the quality
which guarantees
all others.

SIR WINSTON CHURCHILL 1874 – 1965

Y ou gotta stick it out,
because there's only
one ball-game here,
and it's your own life.
You got no choice.
You got to play
to win if you want to
stay on this earth.

CANCER PATIENT

We may encounter many defeats,
but we must not be defeated.

MAYA ANGELOU 1928 – 2014

Courage is fear holding on
a minute longer.

GENERAL GEORGE S. PATTON 1885 – 1945

Anything's possible
if you've got enough nerve.

J. K. ROWLING, B. 1965

Life will break you. Nobody can protect you from that, and living alone won't either, for solitude will also break you with its yearning. You have to love. You have to feel. It is the reason you are here on earth. You are here to risk your heart. You are here to be swallowed up. And when it happens that you are broken, or betrayed, or left, or hurt, or death brushes near, let yourself sit by an apple tree and listen to the apples falling all around you in heaps, wasting their sweetness. Tell yourself you tasted as many as you could.

LOUISE ERDRICH, B. 1954

*All our dreams
can come true
if we have the courage
to pursue them.*

WALT DISNEY 1901 – 1966